RETURNS   Items must be returned or renewed on or before closing time on the last date marked above

RENEWALS   Unless required by other members, items may be renewed at the loaning library in person, or by post or telephone, on two occasions only.

INFORMATION   Member's card number.
NEEDED:

MEMBERSHIP   Please notify any change of name or address.

BOOK CARE   Please look after this item. You may be charged for any damage.

You Have Been Warned!

OXFORD
UNIVERSITY PRESS

Great Clarendon Street, Oxford OX2 6DP

Oxford University Press is a department of the University of Oxford.
It furthers the University's objective of excellence in research, scholarship,
and education by publishing worldwide in

Oxford   New York

Auckland   Cape Town   Dar es Salaam   Hong Kong   Karachi
Kuala Lumpur   Madrid   Melbourne   Mexico City   Nairobi
New Delhi   Shanghai   Taipei   Toronto
With offices in
Argentina   Austria   Brazil   Chile   Czech Republic   France   Greece
Guatemala   Hungary   Italy   Japan   Poland   Portugal   Singapore
South Korea   Switzerland   Thailand   Turkey   Ukraine   Vietnam

Oxford is a registered trade mark of Oxford University Press
in the UK and in certain other countries

British Library Cataloguing in Publication Data
Data available

ISBN: 978-0-19-279216-7

1 3 5 7 9 10 8 6 4 2

Printed in China
Paper used in the production of this book is a natural,
recyclable product made from wood grown in sustainable forests.
The manufacturing process conforms to the environmental
regulations of the country of origin.

You Have Been Warned!
A Collection of Cautionary Verse

chosen by
Roger McGough

illustrated by **Chris Mould**

OXFORD
UNIVERSITY PRESS

Contents

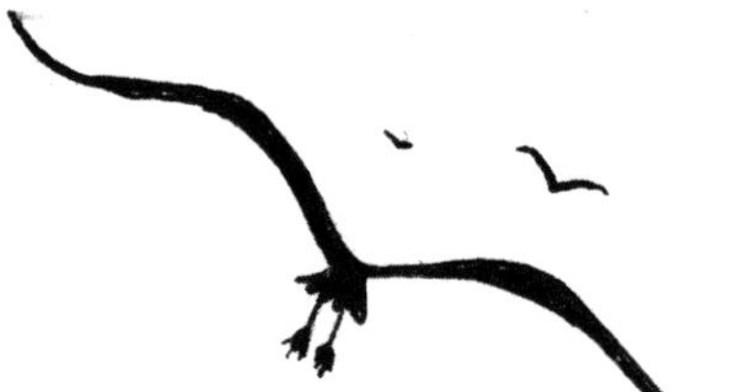

Cautionary Tale

A little girl called Josephine
Was fair of face and reasonably clean
But at school she wore a dunce's cap
And her father, taking out a map

Said: 'She'll learn more if she comes with me
About the world and life at sea.
What she needs is a trip on my schooner
I'm surprised I didn't think of it sooner.

For I'm captain of the *Hesperus*
And I think I know what's best for us.'
And thereupon a most dreadful fate
Befell her, which I'll now relate.

It was winter when they left the port
(in retrospect they shouldn't ought)
Setting sail for the Spanish Main
Despite warnings of a hurricane.

Three days out there came the gale
Even the skipper he turned pale
And as for little Josephine
She turned seven shades of green.

As the schooner rocked from port to starboard
Across the decks poor Josie scarpered
She ran from the fo'c'sle to the stern
(Some folks'll never learn)

Crying: 'Stop the boat, I want to go home,'
But unheeding, the angry foam
Swamped the decks. Her dad did curse
Knowing things would go from bad to worse.

He called his daughter to his side,
'Put on my seaman's coat,' he cried,
'You'll be safe till storm has passed,'
Then bound her tightly to the mast.

And pass it did, but sad to say
Not for a fortnight and a day.
By then the ship had foundered
And all the crew had drownded.

And reported later in the press
Was a story that caused much distress
Of a couple walking on the shore
And of the dreadful sight they saw:

Tied to a mast, a few bones picked clean
All that remained of poor Josephine.

MORAL

Stay on at school, get your GCSEs
Let others sail the seven seas.

Roger McGough

Little Billee

There were three sailors of Bristol city
Who took a boat and went to sea.
But first with beef and captain's biscuits
And pickled pork they loaded she.

There was gorging Jack and guzzling Jimmy,
And the youngest he was little Billee.
Now when they got as far as the Equator
They'd nothing left but one split pea.

Says gorging Jack to guzzling Jimmy,
'I am extremely hungaree.'
To gorging Jack says guzzling Jimmy,
'We've nothing left, us must eat we.'

Says gorging Jack to guzzling Jimmy,
'With one another we shouldn't agree!
There's little Bill, he's younger and tender,
We're old and tough, so let's eat he.

'Oh! Billy, we're going to kill and eat you,
So undo the button of your chemie.'
When Bill received this information
He used his pocket handkerchie.

'First let me say my catechism,
Which my poor mammy taught to me.'
'Make haste, make haste,' says guzzling Jimmy,
While Jack pulled out his snickersnee.

So Billy went up to the maintop gallant mast,
And down he fell on his bended knee.
He scarce had come to the twelfth commandment
When up he jumps. 'There's land I see:

'Jerusalem and Madagascar,
And North and South Amerikee:
There's the British flag a-riding at anchor,
With Admiral Napier, KCB.'

So when they got aboard of the Admiral's
He hanged fat Jack and flogged Jimmee;
But as for little Bill he made him
The Captain of a Seventy-three.

William Makepeace Thackeray

The Canoe-Builder

There was a young man from Crewe,
Who wanted to build a canoe;
He went to the river
And found with a shiver
He hadn't used waterproof glue.

Lorna Bain

Sun, Sand and Sea *or*
Do Have A Nice Day At The Beach

(a poem of advice for a younger brother or sister who's going for a day out by the sea when you're not)

Although I'm ill and stuck indoors,
I hope you have a good day out.
You mustn't let my day spoil yours
As you all gaily play about.

For it's your first time by the sea,
So do enjoy the sand and sun,
But first hear this advice from me
To keep you safe while having fun.

The sun, though safe enough inland,
Is treacherous when at the coast,
So keep your coat on, by the strand,
Or else end up like crispy toast.

The sand: walk on it if you dare,
In shoes that have the thickest treads,
Or broken glass that's hidden there
Will quickly rip your feet to shreds.

The sea, although it seems quite calm,
Can swiftly sweep you far from shore.
The dolt who doubts its deadly harm,
And swims, will soon be seen no more.

Beware the lurking Jellyfish,
Its tentacles and lethal sting.
If slow and painful death's your wish,
The Jellyfish is just the thing.

And mind the Shallow-Paddler-Shark,
Which, searching round for things to eat
And finding you an easy mark,
Will neatly bite off both your feet.

Be wary of the Hairy Grampus
As it lumbers from the spray,
Attracted by the picnic hampers,
Crushing all things in its way.

And don't forget to watch the skies
In case the Red-Beaked Carrion Gull
Should swoop down and peck out your eyes
And rip your face right off your skull.

For many, many are the fools
Who've been on seaside holidays,
And failing to observe these rules,
All died in ghastly, grisly ways.

But though I'm stuck at home in bed,
I'm glad that you can go and play.
Just follow all these things I've said,
And have a happy, carefree day.

David Bateman

Government Health Warning

The boy stood on the burning desk,
Whence all but he had fled,
He tried to quench the flames with ink
(Which happened to be red);

The fire brigade came rushing round,
With ladders, hose and men:
They tried to reach the stricken lad
But flames roared up again.

'Oh help me, please. Oh help me!'
He cried in grief and pain;
'Just get me out; I promise you
I'll never smoke again!'

The firemen they came running
And grabbed the little fool:
And soon he stood there safe and sound
Outside the blazing school.

His friends all gathered round and said:
'Thank God you're in one piece!
We thought they'd never get you out!
Will wonders never cease?'

But then a look of horror ran
Across the young lad's brow;
'I've left a pack of Marlboros there
I don't half need one now!'

Before the watchers scarce could move
Or even cry in fright;
He dashed into the flames again,
And vanished from their sight.

The flames leapt up, and caught the roof,
And down in dust it fell:
And never did they see again
The boy whose tale I tell.

So heed my words, and listen well
If you would live in wealth:
For smoking isn't just a joke.
It *damages* your health!

Christopher Mann

Risk Assessment—Class Outing to Woods
(Based on actual risk assessment forms!)

(Children really must beware —
        Of all the dangerous things out there)
Underfoot, there may be stones:
        Risk of tripping; broken bones.
Climbing over low stone wall:
        Foot could slip and cause a fall.
If weather turns from dry to drippy:
        Mud might make the going slippy.
Patch of nettles:
        Minor harm may be caused to leg or arm.
Meadow, long with grass and clover:
        No running! Risk of falling over.
Enter wood, uneven ground:
        Issue warning—path unsound.
Near to our perambulation:
        Barbed wire—risk of laceration.
Touching leaf-mould, earth and worms:
        Advise against and warn of germs.

So much injury to fear:
        Perhaps we'd better stay right here.
Risk assessment: too many 'shoulds'
        For a simple walk in the local woods.

        Polly Peters

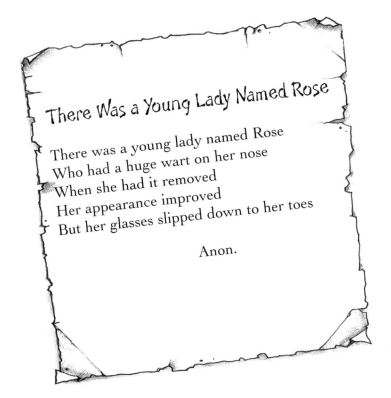

There Was a Young Lady Named Rose

There was a young lady named Rose
Who had a huge wart on her nose
When she had it removed
Her appearance improved
But her glasses slipped down to her toes

Anon.

Just for Fun

It started with a cactus
From a boot sale, just for fun,
But the cactus looked so lonely
That she bought another one,
Then another, then a cheese plant,
Then some fuchsias, then a fern,
Till Belinda's rooms were bursting—
There was hardly room to turn.

Aspidistras, palms, geraniums, lilies—
More and more and more,
Jasmine creeping through the bathroom,
Ivy trailing on the floor,
'Oooh, how lovely!' said the neighbours,
'It's the prettiest house we've seen.'
'Take some cuttings,' said Belinda,
'We can turn the whole street green.'

Soon each house was like a garden,
Tendrils twined themselves in knots,
Climbed the stairs, explored the attics,
Burst like smoke from chimney pots,
Roots went rootling through the cellars,
Shoots went shooting everywhere,
Huge leaves shouldered up the roof tiles
And escaped into the air.

Down the high street, past the station,
Moved the jungle like a tide,
Chasing shoppers out of Tesco's,
Shoving cars and trucks aside,
Swamping parks, devouring statues,
Rolling on and on and on,
Till the last grey wall was swallowed
And the last grey roof was gone.

First arrivals were some fruit bats,
Then a parakeet flew down
And the howls of monkeys echoed
Round what once had been a town.
Tigers prowl the crumbling ruins,
Tree snakes slither in the sun . . .
And all because Belinda
Bought a cactus, just for fun.

Richard Edwards

Robert Jobbins

Robert Jobbins, known as Bobby,
Had the most unusual hobby.
What, you ask, did he collect?
Not, I say, what you'd expect.
No, it wasn't stamps or suchlike.
Bobby's hobby wasn't much like
Any of the usual sort
That perhaps you might have thought.
'How we wish he had another
Hobby,' said his dad and mother
While they watched, with sighs and groans,
As their son collected . . . stones.
Stones of every size and fashion
Were his all-consuming passion.
Not a stone could Bobby pass,
By the roadside, in the grass.
Every single time he found one —
Big or little, square or round one,
Grey or brown or black or white,
Heavy rubble, pebble light —
Bobby took it home to add it
To the other stones he had. It
All provided endless joy
For the Jobbins' little boy.
Soon the fruits of Bobby's labours
Were apparent to the neighbours

As above the Jobbins' wall
There arose a heap so tall
Of these stones and rocks and boulders,
First as high as Bobby's shoulders,
Then, as the collection grew,
Blocking out the neighbours' view,
Rearing up towards the sky, a
Mountain rising ever higher.
Still did little Bobby roam,
Still he brought his prizes home,
Still in vertical direction
Rose and rose his stone collection.
'How much higher, d'you suppose?'
Said his father. 'Heaven knows,'
Said his mother. 'It's a pity,
For our garden once was pretty —
Roses, lupins, hollyhocks —
Now it's just a pile of rocks,
Nothing else but stones is in it
And it's growing by the minute.'
Grow it did till one fine day,
I am sad to have to say —
While the family were gazing
Upwards at that most amazing
Hill of stones of which you've heard —
That an avalanche occurred.
First there was a warning rumble,
Then the stones began to tumble.

None of them was left alive.
Not a Jobbins could survive.
Mum and Dad and little Bobby
Buried under Bobby's hobby.

Dick King-Smith

Screamin' Millie

Millie McDeevit screamed a scream
So loud it made her eyebrows steam.
She screamed so loud her jawbone broke,
Her tongue caught fire, her nostrils smoked,
Her eyeballs boiled and then popped out,
Her ears flew north, her nose went south,
Her teeth flew out, her voice was wrecked,
Her head went sailing off her neck—
Over the hillside, 'cross the stream,
Into the skies it chased the scream.
And that's what happened to Millie McDeevit
(At least I hope all you screamers believe it).

Shel Silverstein

The Boom-Boom-Boom from Susan's Room
(which finally grew too loud to bear)

When parents cup their ears and frown
And scream: 'Child! Turn your music down!'
Most shout in vain. Their words just drown
While house-walls tremble all round town
And chimneys sway and lampposts shake
And those who'd sleep are kept awake
Mistaking it for an earthquake
As pictures fall and mirrors break
And flowers wilt which were in bloom
And doom and gloom appear to loom
And all because twin speakers boom
From in a teenager's bedroom.

But there was once one case much worse,
A din so dangerous and perverse
That no exploding universe
Nor any Hellish devil's curse
Could ever hope to sound as bad.
The rock that roared from Susan's pad
Left neighbours dead or deaf or mad.
There's never been a room that's had
So many speakers stuffed in it
And while they blared, she'd sit and hit
Like in an epileptic fit
The loudest bits of her drum-kit.

'Our Susan's odd,' her parents said
'Because she once fell out of bed
And hit her head and bled and bled
And turned her bedroom carpet red.
Since then she's never played with toys
And isn't interested in boys.
In fact, there's nothing she enjoys
Apart from making loads of noise.
We say: "Find friends." She never heeds.
She won't watch TV, seldom reads.
Loudspeakers now are all she needs
And drums and loads of speaker-leads.'

One day, by way of booster packs,
She raised the row to a new max
And played one of her loudest tracks
And, as it reached its mad climax,
Roof-slates tumbled, windows smashed,
Whole house-bricks crumbled, mortar mashed.
Her parents fled, both bruised and gashed,
And then the entire building crashed . . .
But once that weight had downward rushed
The neighbourhood seemed strangely shushed
Because, beneath, poor Sue lay crushed,
Her and her music wholly hushed.

Be warned, then, if you're in your teens.
Play your rock music by all means,
But speakers packed in like sardines
Will smash you into smithereens.

Nick Toczek

Headphone Harold

Headphone Harold wore his headphones
Through the night and through the day.
He said, 'I'd rather hear my music
Than the dumb things people say.'

In the city's honkin' traffic,
He heard trumpets 'stead of trucks.
Down the quiet country back roads
He heard drums instead of ducks.

Through the patterin' springtime showers
He heard guitars instead of rain.
Down the track at the railroad crossin'
He heard the trombones—not the *train*.

Shel Silverstein

Ear Popping

To blow your ears clear
hold your nose.
And with a POP
the blockage goes.
But please remember,
pay regard.
Never blow too long
or hard.
I knew a boy
who didn't stop
when at first
he heard no POP.
He blew until
his face turned red
and POPPED the ears
clear off his head!

Jez Alborough

Llewelyn Peter James Maguire

Llewelyn Peter James Maguire,
Touched a live electric wire;
Back on his heels it sent him rocking—
His language (like the wire) was shocking.

Harry Graham

Ten Little Schoolboys

Ten little schoolboys went out to dine;
One choked his little self, and then there were nine.

Nine little schoolboys sat up very late;
One overslept himself, and then there were eight.

Eight little schoolboys travelling to Devon;
One said he'd stay there, and then there were seven.

Seven little schoolboys chopping up sticks;
One chopped himself in half and then there were six.

Six little schoolboys playing with a hive;
A bumble bee stung one, and then there were five.

Five little schoolboys going in for law;
One got in chancery, and then there were four.

Four little schoolboys going out to sea;
A red herring swallowed one, and then there were three.

Three little schoolboys walking in the zoo;
A big bear hugged one, and then there were two.

Two little schoolboys sitting in the sun;
One got frizzled up, and then there was one.

One little schoolboy living all alone;
He got married, and then there was none.

Anon.

The Boy with a Similar Name

When Raymond Gough joined our class
He was almost a year behind.
'Sanitorium,' said Mrs McBride,
'So I want you all to be kind.'

'Roger, your names are similar
So let Raymond sit next to you.
He'll need a friend to teach him the ropes
And show him what to do.'

Then teacher went back to teaching
And we went back to being taught
And I tried to be kind to Raymond
But it was harder than I thought.

For he was the colour of candlewax
And smelled of Dettol and Vick.
He was as thin as a sharpened pencil
And his glasses were milkbottle thick.

Not only that but unfriendly
All muffled up in his shell.
Hobbies? Interests? Ambitions?
It was impossible to tell.

I was afraid of catching his yellowness
And smelling of second-hand Vick
And the only time I could be myself
Were the days when he was off sick.

But what proved to be contagious
Was his oddness, and I knew
That he was a victim ripe for bullying
And so by proxy, I was too.

'How's your brother Raymond?'
The class began to tease,
'Do you share his dirty handkerchief?
Do you catch each other's fleas?'

'He's not my brother,' I shouted,
My cheeks all burning hot,
'He's a drippy, four-eyed monster,
And he comes from the planet Snot.'

They laughed, and I saw an opening
(Wouldn't you have done the same?)
I pointed a finger at Raymond
And joined in the bullying game.

He stopped coming to school soon after,
'Sanitorium,' said Mrs McBride.
He never came back and nobody knew
If he moved elsewhere or died.

I don't think of him very often
For when I do I blush with shame
At the thought of the pain I helped inflict
On the boy with a similar name.

Roger McGough

A Little Mistake

I studied my tables over and over, and backward and
    forward, too;
But I couldn't remember six times nine, and I didn't know
    what to do,
Till sister told me to play with my doll, and not to bother
    my head.
'If you call her "Fifty-four" for a while, you'll learn it by heart,'
    she said.

So I took my favourite Mary Ann (though I thought 'twas a
    dreadful shame
To give such a perfectly lovely child such a perfectly
    horrid name),
And I called her my dear little 'Fifty-four' a hundred times,
    till I knew
The answer of six times nine as well as the answer to two
    times two.

Next day, Elizabeth Wigglesworth, who always seemed so
    proud,
Said, 'Six times nine is fifty-two,' and I nearly laughed aloud!
But I wished I hadn't when teacher said, 'Now, Dorothy,
    tell if you can,'
For I thought of my doll, and—oh dear me!—I answered
    'Mary Ann!'

Anna M. Pratt

My Sneaky Cousin

She put in her clothes,
Then thought she'd get
A free bath here
At the launderette.
So round she goes now,
Flippity-flappy,
Lookin' clean—
But not too happy.

Shel Silverstein

Cautionary Playground Rhyme

Natasha Green
Natasha Green
stuck her head in a washing machine

Washing Machine
Washing Machine
round and round Natasha Green

Natasha Green
Natasha Green
cleanest girl I've ever seen

Ever Seen
Ever Seen
a girl with her head in a washing machine?

Washing Machine
Washing Machine
last home of Natasha Green

Natasha Green
Natasha Green
washed away in a white machine

White Machine
White Machine
soaped to death Natasha Green

Natasha Green
Natasha Green
cleanest ghost I've ever seen!

MORAL:

Washing machines are for knickers and blouses
Washing machines are for jumpers and trousers
Keep your head out of the washing machine
or you'll end up as spotless as little Miss Green.

Ian McMillan

Stock Cupboard Rap

In our teacher's stock cupboard
With his paper and pens,
Lurk all sorts
Of his peculiar friends.

Large and small, fat and thin,
You'd better watch out if you need to go in!

There's a little brown hairy one
That lives on the floor,
And will bite your leg
When you come through the door!

Large and small, fat and thin,
You'd better watch out if you need to go in!

The long thin furry one
Sits on the shelf,
Show him a mirror
And he'd frighten himself!

Large and small, fat and thin,
You'd better watch out if you need to go in!

The teeny black fuzzy one
Hides among the pens,
With fangs like that
He hasn't many friends!

Large and small, fat and thin,
You'd better watch out if you need to go in!

But the hairiest, scariest creature of all
Clings like a limpet up on the wall.
When you creep inside he stretches his limbs,
And tickles your head, among other things!

Large and small, fat and thin,
You'd better watch out if you need to go in!

So take great care if you have to find
A pencil, a rubber or a pen of some kind.
To go in that cupboard takes nerves of steel,
Cos if one doesn't get you—
ANOTHER ONE WILL!!

Anne Logan

Be Very Afraid

of the Spotted Pyjama Spider
which disguises itself as a spot
on the sleeve of your nightwear,
waits till you fall asleep,
then commences its ominous creep
towards your face.

Be very afraid
of the Hanging Lightcord Snake
which waits in the dark
for your hand to reach for the switch,
then wraps itself round your wrist
with a venomous hiss. Be afraid,

very afraid, of the Toothpaste Worm
which is camouflaged as a stripe of red
in the paste you squeeze
and oozes onto your brush
with a wormy guile
to squirm on your smile.

Be very afraid indeed
of the Bookworm Bat
which wraps itself like a dust-jacket
over a book,
then flaps and squeaks in your face
when you take a look. Be afraid

of the Hairbrush Rat, of the Merit Badge Beetle,
of the Bubble Bath Jellyfish
and the Wrist Watch Tick (with its terrible nip),
of the Sock Wasp, of the Bee in the Bonnet
(posed as an amber jewel
in the hatpin on it). Be feart

of the Toilet Roll Scorpion,
snug as a bug in its cardboard tube
until someone disturbs it,
of the Killer Earring Ant,
dangling from a lobe
until someone perturbs it. Don't be brave —

be very afraid.

Carol Ann Duffy

Willie White

A little boy called Willie White
Would never go to sleep at night.
'I'm frightened of the dark,' he said
Each evening when he went to bed,
'So leave the light on if you will
And do not turn it off until
The nasty night has gone away.'
Then Willie White would sleep all day
Until at last they brought a plate
Of breakfast. This was served at eight
P.M. He had his lunch at one
A.M. His supper was begun
At dawn. And then, once it was light,
Straight off to sleep went Willie White.
Then came the day when Willie had
To go to school. The little lad
Was weary as could be because
He hadn't slept. No sooner was
He in his seat on that first morn
Than Willie White began to yawn,
And next he lay upon the floor
And very soon began to snore.
'What's up?' his teacher then enquired
Of Mrs White. 'Our Willie's tired,'
She said. 'The reason's plain, I think —
Last night he never slept a wink.'
Thereafter it became the rule

As soon as Willie got to school
He'd fall into an instant sleep.
So heavy was it and so deep
That it was useless, that was plain,
To try to wake him up again.
The other children learned to read
And do the things that children need,
Like sums, and learning how to write
And draw and paint, which Willie White
Could not be taught to understand
Because he was in slumberland.
And so he never learned a jot
But ended up a perfect clot
Who couldn't read or write or do
A simple sum like two plus two.
I do not think that you can fail
To see the moral of this tale.
Don't be like silly Willie White,
But always go to sleep AT NIGHT.

Dick King-Smith

Mother Goblin's Lullaby

Go to sleep, my baby goblin,
hushaby, my dear of dears,
if you disobey your mother,
she will twist your pointed ears.

Little goblin, stop complaining,
time for all your eyes to close,
if you make your mother angry,
she will bite your tiny nose.

Slumber sweetly till tomorrow,
do not worry, Mother's near,
dream of demons weirdly screaming,
hushaby, my goblin dear.

                                        Jack Prelutsky

Story of Little Suck-a-Thumb

One day Mamma said 'Conrad dear,
I must go out and leave you here.
But mind now, Conrad, what I say,
Don't suck your thumb while I'm away.
The great tall tailor always comes

To little boys who suck their thumbs;
And ere they dream what he's about,
He takes his great sharp scissors out,
And cuts their thumbs clean off—and then,
You know, they never grow again.'

Mamma had scarcely turned her back,
The thumb was in, Alack! Alack!
The door flew open, in he ran,
The great, long, blue-legged scissor-man.
Oh! children, see! the tailor's come
And caught out little Suck-a-Thumb.
Snip! Snap! Snip! the scissors go;
And Conrad cried out 'Oh! Oh! Oh!'
Snip! Snap! Snip! They go so fast,
That both his thumbs are off at last.

Mamma comes home: there Conrad stands,
And looks quite sad, and shows his hands;
'Ah!' said Mamma, 'I knew he'd come
To naughty little Suck-a-Thumb.'

Dr Heinrich Hoffmann

Jimmy Jet and his TV Set

I'll tell you the story of Jimmy Jet—
And you know what I tell you is true.
He loved to watch his TV set
Almost as much as you.

He watched all day, he watched all night
Till he grew pale and lean,
From 'The Early Show' to 'The Late Late Show'
And all the shows between.

He watched till his eyes were frozen wide,
And his bottom grew into his chair.
And his chin turned into a tuning dial,
And antennae grew out of his hair.

And his brains turned into TV tubes,
And his face to a TV screen,
And two knobs saying 'VERT.' and 'HORIZ.'
Grew where his ears had been.

And he grew a plug that looked like a tail
So we plugged in little Jim.
And now instead of him watching TV
We all sit around and watch him.

Shel Silverstein

Teevee

In the house
of Mr and Mrs Spouse
he and she
would watch teevee
and never a word
between them spoken
until the day
the set was broken.

Then 'How do you do?'
said he to she,
'I don't believe
that we've met yet.
Spouse is my name.
What's yours?' he asked.

'Why, mine's the same!'
she said to he,
'Do you suppose that we could be—?'

But the set came suddenly right about,
and so they never did find out.

Eve Merriam

Sid the Skateboarder

Skate-boarder Sid! His skill was wow!
He was, like, cool, *and man,* like how!
Like, scary, *see, like* REAL Xtreme!
He did things others never dream!
It's true, I saw him down South Bank
Flying over the taxi rank,
No helmet, no pads, as if the air
Were any devil's for a dare.
        So what went wrong? Ridiculous,
He should end up like Icarus,
(That's Daedalus's smartass kid
who also fell to earth, like Sid,
someone you ought to know about,
go find a book and check it out.)
In any case, where was I? Yes,
Now I remember, more or less.

Sid, and the all-time US champ,
Were working up speed down the ramp
When Sid's board hit a greasy spot.
Accelerated thus, Sid shot
Beyond the city's limits, through
Long miles and miles of soft blurred blue
Diving headlong into the sea
A little beyond Pevensey,
Like Icarus, a falling star.
And wow! Like man, way out! Too far!
Like, yeah, you know, like he skateboarded
Where records haven't been recorded.
Don't follow Sid, dude. Know what's hot,
And look out for that greasy spot!

George Szirtes

54

Icarus

With wax and feathers
just for fun
he tried to fly up to the sun.
'The wax is melting!'
(came a shout
as all his feathers fluttered out).

He fell to the ground
the end of Icarus . . .
inventive
brave
but quite ridiculous.

Peter Dixon

Icarus Schmicarus

If you never spend your money
you know you'll always have some cash
If you stay cool and never burn
you'll never turn to ash
If you lick the boots that kick you
then you'll never feel the lash
And if you crawl along the ground
at least you'll never crash
So why why why—
WHAT MADE YOU THINK YOU COULD FLY?

Adrian Mitchell

See a pin and pick it up.
See a pin and pick it up,
All the day you'll have good luck
See a pin and let it lie,
You'll be sorry by and by.

Anon.

A thrifty young fellow of Shoreham

A thrifty young fellow of Shoreham
Made brown paper trousers, and wore 'em.
He looked nice and neat,
Till he bent in the street
To pick up a pin, then he tore 'em.

Anon.

Charity

While once in haste I crossed the street,
  A little girl I saw,
Deep in the mud she'd placed her feet,
  And gazed on me with awe.

'Dear sir,' with trembling tone she said,
  'Here have I stood for weeks,
And never had a bit of bread,'
  Here tears bedewed her cheeks.

'Poor child!' said I, 'do you stand here,
  And quickly will I buy
Some wholesome bread and strengthening beer,
  And fetch it speedily.'

Off ran I to the baker's shop,
  As hard as I could pelt,
Fearing 'twas late, I made a stop,
  And in my pocket felt.

In my left pocket did I seek,
  To see how time went on,
Then grief and tears bedewed *my* cheek,
  For oh! my watch was gone!

                Lewis Carroll

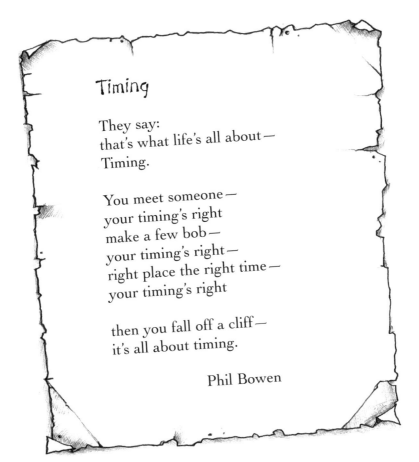

Timing

They say:
that's what life's all about—
Timing.

You meet someone—
your timing's right
make a few bob—
your timing's right—
right place the right time—
your timing's right

then you fall off a cliff—
it's all about timing.

Phil Bowen

I Found a Four-Leaf Clover

I found a four-leaf clover
and was happy with my find,
but with time to think it over,
I've entirely changed my mind.
I concealed it in my pocket,
safe inside a paper pad,
soon, much swifter than a rocket,
my good fortune turned to bad.

I smashed my fingers in a door,
I dropped a dozen eggs,
I slipped and tumbled to the floor,
a dog nipped both my legs,
my ring slid down the bathtub drain,
my pen leaked on my shirt,
I barked my shin, I missed my train,
I sat on my dessert.

I broke my brand-new glasses,
and I couldn't find my keys,
I stepped in spilled molasses,
and was stung by angry bees.
When the kitten ripped the curtain,
and the toast burst into flame,
I was absolutely certain
that the clover was to blame.

I buried it discreetly
in the middle of a field,
now my luck has changed completely,
and my wounds have almost healed.
If I ever find another,
I will simply let it be,
or I'll give it to my brother —
he deserves it more than me.

Jack Prelutsky

Lucky

There was a boy at school we called 'Lucky'
    All he did was whinge and moan
'Lucky' was the nickname we gave him
    Because he was so accident-prone

If something was spilled or knocked over
    Splattered, burnt or bust
There in the midst of the damage
    Would be Lucky looking nonplussed

He said that bad things happened to him
    Having been born under an unlucky star
And a fortune-teller warned his mother
    Not to let him travel far

So to ward off every kind of harm
    The gypsy gave him a lucky charm:
A silver horseshoe, rabbit's paw,
    Lucky heather, eagle's claw,
Coloured glass and polished stones
    Dried hair and yellowing bones

He never walked under ladders
    Never stepped on pavement cracks
Never touched a looking-glass
    Never learned how to relax

You could spot Lucky a mile off
    Count the creases in his frown
As he concentrated on keeping alive
    His pockets weighted down

With a silver horseshoe, rabbit's paw,
    Lucky heather, eagle's claw,
Coloured glass and polished stones
    Dried hair and yellowing bones

Though the streets were full of happy kids
    He was never allowed out to play
In case of bombs, or tigers, or ghosts
    So he stayed in, out of harm's way

Then one afternoon his luck changed
    (Friday the Thirteenth, coincidentally)
He'd been kept in detention after school
    For setting fire to it (accidentally)

When hurrying home and touching wood
    For it was then well after dark
Three lads jumped him, mugged him
    Took all he had, near the gates of the park

A silver horseshoe, rabbit's paw,
    Lucky heather, eagle's claw,
Coloured glass and polished stones
    Dried hair and yellowing bones

Lucky laid low and cowered for days
    As if some tragedy would befall
But nothing unusual happened
    Nothing. Simply nothing at all

It was as if he'd been living underwater
    And at last had come up for air
Then the following week his dad won the pools
    And became a millionaire

We never saw Lucky after that
　　The family moved out to Australia
So the moral is: Chuck them away
　　Or doomed you'll be to failure

A silver horseshoe, rabbit's paw,
*　　Lucky heather, eagle's claw,*
Coloured glass and polished stones
*　　Dried hair and yellowing bones*

Roger McGough

George Who Played with a Dangerous Toy, and Suffered a Catastrophe of Considerable Dimensions

When George's Grandmamma was told
That George had been as good as Gold,
She Promised in the Afternoon
To buy him an *Immense* BALLOON.
And so she did; but when it came,
It got into the candle flame,
And being of a dangerous sort
Exploded with a Loud Report!
The Lights went out! The Windows broke!
The Room was filled with reeking smoke!
And in the darkness shrieks and yells
Were mingled with Electric Bells,
And falling masonry and groans,
And crunching, as of broken bones,
And dreadful shrieks, when, worst of all,
The House itself began to fall!
It tottered, shuddering to and fro,
Then crashed into the street below—
Which happened to be Savile Row.

When Help arrived, among the Dead
Were Cousin Mary, Little Fred,
The Footmen (both of them), the Groom,
The man that cleaned the Billiard-Room,
The Chaplain, and the Still-Room Maid.

And I am dreadfully afraid
That Monsieur Champignon, the Chef,
Will now be permanently deaf—
And both his Aides are much the same;
While George, who was in part to blame,
Received, you will regret to hear,
A nasty lump behind his ear.

The moral is that little Boys
Should not be given dangerous Toys.

Hilaire Belloc

The Lion and Albert

There's a famous seaside place called Blackpool,
That's noted for fresh air and fun,
And Mr and Mrs Ramsbottom
Went there with young Albert, their son.

A grand little lad was young Albert,
All dressed in his best; quite a swell
With a stick with an 'orse's 'ead 'andle,
The finest that Woolworth's could sell.

They didn't think much to the Ocean:
The waves, they was fiddlin' and small,
There was no wrecks and nobody drownded,
Fact, nothing to laugh at at all.

So, seeking for further amusement,
They paid and went into the Zoo,
Where they'd Lions and Tigers and Camels,
And old ale and sandwiches too.

There were one great big Lion called Wallace;
His nose were all covered with scars—
He lay in a somnolent posture,
With the side of his face on the bars.

Now Albert had heard about Lions,
How they was ferocious and wild—
To see Wallace lying so peaceful,
Well, it didn't seem right to the child.

So straightway the brave little feller,
Not showing a morsel of fear,
Took his stick with its 'orse's 'ead 'andle
And pushed it in Wallace's ear.

You could see that the Lion didn't like it,
For giving a kind of a roll,
He pulled Albert inside the cage with 'im,
And swallowed the little lad 'ole.

Then Pa, who had seen the occurrence,
And didn't know what to do next,
Said, 'Mother! Yon Lion's 'et Albert,'
And Mother said, 'Well, I am vexed!'

Then Mr and Mrs Ramsbottom—
Quite rightly, when all's said and done—
Complained to the Animal Keeper,
That the Lion had eaten their son.

The keeper was quite nice about it;
He said, 'What a nasty mishap.
Are you sure that it's *your* boy he's eaten?'
Pa said, 'Am I sure? There's his cap!'

The manager had to be sent for.
He came and said, 'What's to do?'
Pa said, 'Yon Lion's 'et Albert,
And 'im in his Sunday clothes, too.'

Then Mother said, 'Right's right, young feller;
I think it's a shame and a sin,
For a lion to go and eat Albert,
And after we've paid to come in.'

The manager wanted no trouble,
He took out his purse right away,
Saying, 'How much to settle the matter?'
And Pa said, 'What do you usually pay?'

But Mother had turned a bit awkward
When she thought where her Albert had gone.
She said, 'No! someone's got to be summonsed'—
So that was decided upon.

Then off they went to the P'lice Station,
In front of the Magistrate chap;
They told 'im what happened to Albert,
And proved it by showing his cap.

The Magistrate gave his opinion
That no one was really to blame
And he said that he hoped the Ramsbottoms
Would have further sons to their name.

At that Mother got proper blazing,
'And thank you, sir, kindly,' said she.
'What waste all our lives raising children
To feed ruddy Lions? Not me!'

Marriott Edgar

A Fable

A crazy hunter, following a bear,
And pressing harder than a man should dare,
Was menaced by a leopard and a lion.
Availed no prayer, no cries to Heaven or Zion,
For he had slain their cubs, and with vile blows,
And welded Sky to Jungle by their woes.

Gazing upon a tree, he swiftly fled.
But in his path the bear with turning tread
Firm hindered the supposed security.
Oh, what to do? How save himself from three?
Dropping his gun, he howled and beat the air;
Then, stretching wide his arms, embraced the bear.
'Save me, sweet beast!' he cried. 'Love! Lick my face!'
Which the bear did, returning the embrace.

You know the rest, you know the tightening squeeze.
Only to think, it makes your spirit freeze;
Only to think, it pulls you to the ground,
And makes your blood run cold, your head go round.

Moral: To wicked beasts be straight and fair;
But do not pet them. Face them, and beware!
And never drop your gun to hug a bear.

Herbert Palmer

Treasure Trail

Normally
I get home from school
and go straight out again
to the park
but today

I spotted a penny on the hall floor
and as I bent to pick it up
I spotted another —
one pace away

As I bent to pick that up
I spotted another —
one pace away

As I bent to pick that up
I spotted yet another
on the bottom step
of the stairs

I picked it up
and spied another
on the third step

and another on the seventh
and another on the tenth
and another at the top

At the top of the stairs
I spotted a five p
on the landing—
one pace away

At this rate I was going to be rich.
I followed the trail
to the door of my room

The door was open
and I could see
a ten p
on my floor

I went in and,
as I bent to pick it up,
the door slammed shut
behind me.

I tried to open it
but it was shut fast.
A note was pinned to the door

It said, You are my prisoner!
You are not getting out
until you have tidied your room!
Signed
Mum

And all for
Twenty-five p!

Roger Stevens

Rebecca, Who Slammed Doors for Fun and Perished Miserably

A Trick that everyone abhors
In Little Girls is slamming Doors.
A Wealthy Banker's Little Daughter
Who lived in Palace Green, Bayswater
(By name Rebecca Offendort),
Was given to this Furious Sport.

She would deliberately go
And Slam the door like Billy-Ho!
To make her Uncle Jacob start.
She was not really bad at heart,
But only rather rude and wild;
She was an aggravating child.

It happened that a Marble Bust
Of Abraham was standing just
Above the Door this little Lamb
Had carefully prepared to Slam,
And Down it came! It knocked her flat!
It laid her out! She looked like that!

Her Funeral Sermon (which was long
And followed by a Sacred Song)
Mentioned her Virtues, it is true,
But dwelt upon her Vices, too,
And showed the Dreadful End of One
Who goes and slams the Door for Fun.

The children who were brought to hear
The Awful Tale from far and near
Were much impressed, and inly swore
They never more would slam the Door
—As they had often done before.

Hilaire Belloc

The Mistletoe Bough

The mistletoe hung in the castle hall,
The holly branch shone on the old oak wall;
And the baron's retainers were blithe and gay,
And keeping their Christmas holiday.
The baron beheld with a father's pride
His beautiful child, young Lovell's bride;
While she with her bright eyes seem'd to be
The star of the goodly company.

'I'm weary of dancing now;' she cried;
'Here tarry a moment—I'll hide—I'll hide!
And, Lovell, be sure thou'rt first to trace
The clue to my secret lurking place.'
Away she ran—and her friends began
Each tower to search, and each nook to scan;
And young Lovell cried, 'Oh where dost thou hide?
I'm lonesome without thee, my own dear bride.'

They sought her that night! and they sought her
    next day!
And they sought her in vain when a week pass'd away!
In the highest—the lowest—the loneliest spot,
Young Lovell sought wildly—but found her not.
And years flew by, and their grief at last
Was told as a sorrowful tale long past;
And when Lovell appeared, the children cried,
'See! the old man weeps for his fairy bride.'

At length an oak chest, that had long lain hid,
Was found in the castle—they raised the lid—
And a skeleton form lay mouldering there,
In the bridal wreath of that lady fair!
Oh! sad was her fate!—in sportive jest
She hid from her lord in the old oak chest.
It closed with a spring!—and, dreadful doom,
The bride lay clasp'd in her living tomb!

Thomas Haynes Bayly

Sir Guy and the Enchanted Princess

Through howling winds on a storm-tossed moor
Sir Guy came to a castle door.

He was led by some strange power
To the deepest dungeon of a ruined tower.

A Princess sat on a jewelled throne
Her lovely features carved in stone.

Her body trembled, was she dead?
Then her sweet voice filled his head.

'These evil spirits guard me well
Brave Sir Knight, please break their spell.

Though I am stone, you shall see
Kiss me once, I shall be free.'

As demons howled she came to life
Blushed and whispered, 'Have you a wife?'

'My love,' he said, 'still remains
with collecting stamps and spotting trains

But as long as you do as you're told
I think you'll do, come on, it's cold.'

'Oh,' she cried, 'you weedy bore
I wish I was entranced once more.'

Lightning struck, the demons hissed
Sir Guy was stone, a voice croaked 'Missed!'

The Princess rode his horse away
And poor Sir Guy's still there today.

David Harmer

Henry My Son

'Where have you been all the day,
Henry my son?
Where have you been all the day,
My handsome one?'

'In the woods, dear Mother.
In the woods, dear Mother.
Oh, Mother, be quick
I'm going to be sick
And lay me down to die.'

'Oh, what did you do in the woods,
Henry my boy?
What did you do in the woods,
My pride and joy?'

'Ate, dear Mother.
Ate, dear Mother.
Oh, Mother, be quick
I'm going to be sick
And lay me down to die.'

'Oh, what did you eat in the woods,
Henry my son?
What did you eat in the woods,
My handsome one?'

'Eels, dear Mother.
Eels, dear Mother.
Oh, Mother, be quick
I'm going to be sick
And lay me down to die.'

'Oh, what colour was them eels,
Henry my boy?
What colour was them eels,
My pride and joy?'

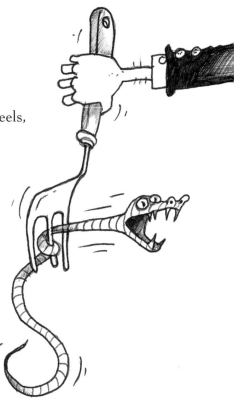

'Green and yeller!
Green and yeller!
Oh, Mother, be quick
I'm going to be sick
And lay me down to die.'

'Them eels was snakes,
Henry my son.
Them eels was snakes,
My handsome one.'

'Yerr-uck! dear Mother.
Yerr-uck! dear Mother.
Oh, Mother, be quick
I'm going to be sick
And lay me down to die.'

'Oh, what colour flowers would you like,
Henry my son?
What colour flowers would you like,
My handsome one?'

'Green and yeller.
Green and yeller.
Oh, Mother, be quick
I'm going to be sick
And lay me down to die.'

Anon.

Cy's Mother Said

Cy's mother said
He never should
Eat the pretty berries
Growing in the wood.

But Cy didn't listen,
He ate some for a dare,
Now Cy's in
Intensive care.

Richard Edwards

Where the Blackberries Grow

Blackberries grow by the railway track,
Red and green and juicy black,
But nobody goes by the railway track:
Sadie went there and never came back.
Now nobody goes by the railway track,
Where the blackberries grow so juicy black.

David Greygoose

The Witch! The Witch!

The Witch! the Witch! don't let her get you!
Or your Aunt wouldn't know you the next time
she met you!

Eleanor Farjeon

Look out, boys!

Look out! Look out, boys! Clear the track!
The witches are here! They've all come back!
They hanged them high — No use! No use!
What cares a witch for the hangman's noose?
They buried them deep, but they wouldn't lie still,
For cats and witches are hard to kill;
They swore they shouldn't and wouldn't die —
Books said they did, but they lie! they lie!

Oliver Wendell Holmes

The Tongue-Twister

Watch out for the dreaded Tongue-twister
When he pulls on his surgical gloves.
Keep your eyes open, your mouth tightly shut,
Twisting tongues is the thing that he loves.

It's the slippery, squirmy feel of them
As they wriggle like landed fish.
When he pulls and tugs and grapples
You'll grasp and gurgle and wish

That you'd never pulled tongues at teacher
Or a stranger behind their back,
As he twists out your tongue and pops it
Into his bobbling, twisted-tongue sack.

Roger McGough

The Visitor

A crumbling churchyard, the sea and the moon;
The waves had gouged out grave and bone;
A man was walking, late and alone . . .

He saw a skeleton white on the ground;
A ring on a bony finger he found.

He ran home to his wife and gave her the ring.
'Oh, where did you get it?' He said not a thing.

'It's the prettiest ring in the world,' she said,
As it glowed on her finger. They slipped off to bed.

At midnight they woke. In the dark outside,
'Give me my ring!' a chill voice cried.

'What was that, William? What did it say?'
'Don't worry, my dear. It'll soon go away.'

'I'm coming!' A skeleton opened the door.
'Give me my ring!' It was crossing the floor.

'What was that, William? What did it say?'
'Don't worry, my dear. It'll soon go away.'

'I'm reaching you now! I'm climbing the bed.'
The wife pulled the sheet right over her head.

It was torn from her grasp and tossed in the air:
'I'll drag you out of your bed by the hair!'

'What was that, William? What did it say?'
'Throw the ring through the window! THROW IT
    AWAY!'

She threw it. The skeleton leapt from the sill,
Scooped up the ring and clattered downhill,
Fainter . . . and fainter . . .Then all was still.

Ian Serraillier

Bump!

Things that go 'bump!' in the night,
Should not really give one a fright.
It's the hole in each ear
That lets in the fear,
That, and the absence of light!

Spike Milligan

No Trespassers

Do not explore on Rannoch Moor
as dark descends and spectres roar,
when peat bogs boil and you're alone,
where puking spooks garrotte and groan.

There's shapes that scream on Rannoch Moor,
broad shadow beasts which gouge and gore.
There's bats and rats to drink your veins
And gangly ghouls that swallow trains.

Ogres og on Rannoch Moor —
they must have someone fresh to gnaw,
and things chew eyes and spiders crush
each human being to slurp size mush.

So tremble, fret and be unsure
if you should stray on Rannoch Moor.
Best stay off if you guard your health . . .
 . . . I must keep Rannoch to myself.

Stewart Henderson

from The Spider and the Fly

'Will you walk into my parlour?' said the Spider to the Fly,
'Tis the prettiest little parlour that ever you did spy;
The way into my parlour is up a winding stair,
And I have many curious things to show when you are
     there.'
'Oh no, no,' said the little Fly, 'to ask me is in vain,
For who goes up your winding stair can ne'er come
     down again.'

Mary Howitt

Poor Old Lady

Poor old lady, she swallowed a fly.
I don't know why she swallowed a fly.
Poor old lady, I think she'll die.

Poor old lady, she swallowed a spider.
It squirmed and wriggled and turned inside her.
She swallowed the spider to catch the fly.
I don't know why she swallowed a fly.
Poor old lady, I think she'll die.

Poor old lady, she swallowed a bird.
How absurd! She swallowed a bird.
She swallowed the bird to catch the spider,
She swallowed the spider to catch the fly,
I don't know why she swallowed a fly.
Poor old lady, I think she'll die.

Poor old lady, she swallowed a cat.
Think of that! She swallowed a cat.
She swallowed the cat to catch the bird,
She swallowed the bird to catch the spider,
She swallowed the spider to catch the fly,
I don't know why she swallowed a fly.
Poor old lady, I think she'll die.

Poor old lady, she swallowed a dog.
She went the whole hog when she swallowed the dog.
She swallowed the dog to catch the cat,
She swallowed the cat to catch the bird,
She swallowed the bird to catch the spider,
She swallowed the spider to catch the fly,
I don't know why she swallowed a fly.
Poor old lady, I think she'll die.

Poor old lady, she swallowed a cow.
I don't know how she swallowed the cow.
She swallowed the cow to catch the dog,
She swallowed the dog to catch the cat,
She swallowed the cat to catch the bird,
She swallowed the bird to catch the spider,
She swallowed the spider to catch the fly,
I don't know why she swallowed a fly.
Poor old lady, I think she'll die.

Poor old lady, she swallowed a horse.
She died, of course.

Anon.

Sybil the Magician's Last Show

Magical Sybil was much too cheap
To buy her rabbit a carrot.
He grew so thin, just bones and skin,
So starved he couldn't bear it —
And so, as she reached into her hat
To grab him by the ears,
She felt a tug, she felt a pull,
And *WHAP*—she disappeared,
'The greatest act we've ever seen,'
We cheered for Magical Sybil.
But all that remained was a hat and a cape
And the sound of a bunny
Goin', 'Nibble . . . nibble . . . nibble.'

Shel Silverstein

The Story of Anthony, the Boy Who Knew Too Much

Anthony, though not unkind,
Had a disbelieving mind.
At a pantomime or play
Anthony would yawn and say,

'Let's go home—for I perceive
This is merely make-believe.'
When his mother came and read
Story-books to him in bed
Anthony would shake his head
'Mother, dear, I've had enough
Of this wishy-washy stuff.
If it's all the same to you
Kindly read me something *true*.'
So his mother, with a sigh,
Meekly laying fiction by,
Read him books about machines,
And scientific magazines.

Christmas time came round once more.
See him sitting on the floor
At a party, after he
Has enjoyed a sumptuous tea.
Solemnly the Conjurer stands
Spreading out his empty hands:
Then from nose and ears he hauls
Half-a-dozen billiard-balls,
Shows them with a smile, and then
Makes them disappear again.
Children clap him with a will:
Only Anthony sits still,
Saying loudly, '*I* believe
That he's got them up his sleeve.'

The Conjurer, who must have heard,
Looked at him, but said no word.

So with all his other tricks:
Flour and butter he would mix
In a bowl, and 'One-two-three!'
There the finished cake would be.
Loud applause—but Anthony
Merely said, 'Well, *I* believe
That he had it up his sleeve.'

Coins he'd find in Susan's hair
Which she didn't know were there;
Handkerchiefs of every hue
He would draw from Edward's shoe,
And produce, as pat as pat,
Rabbits from an empty hat.
All the other girls and boys
Laughed and clapped with merry noise:
But Anthony said, '*I* believe
He had the whole lot up his sleeve.'

The Conjurer politely smiled
At the infuriating child,
And said, 'Come close, my little man,
And learn my secrets if you can.'
Young Anthony marched up with glee
Remarking, 'Huh! You can't catch *me*!'
'Now,' said the great man, '*one-two-three!*'

And Anthony—ah, where was he?
His mother wildly glanced around.
The boy was nowhere to be found:
But in the Conjurer's top-hat
A third and extra rabbit sat . . .

Children, when you go to parties
Never talk like little smarties:
Even if you *don't* believe,
Keep your knowledge up your sleeve.

Jan Struther

There Was a Young Man from Bengal

There was a young man from Bengal
Who went to a fancy dress ball.
He thought he would risk it
And go as a biscuit,
But a dog ate him up in the hall.

Anon.

An Elegy on the Death of a Mad Dog

Good people all, of every sort,
    Give ear unto my song;
And if you find it wondrous short,
    It cannot hold you long.

In Islington there was a man,
    Of whom the world might say,
That still a godly race he ran,
    Whene'er he went to pray.

A kind and gentle heart he had,
    To comfort friends and foes;
The naked every day he clad,
    When he put on his clothes.

And in that town a dog was found,
    As many dogs there be,
Both mongrel, puppy, whelp, and hound,
    And curs of low degree.

This dog and man at first were friends;
    But when a pique began,
The dog, to gain his private ends,
    Went mad, and bit the man.

Around from all the neighbouring streets
    The wondering neighbours ran,
And swore the dog had lost his wits,
    To bite so good a man.

The wound it seemed both sore and sad
    To every Christian eye;
And while they swore the dog was mad,
    They swore the man would die.

But soon a wonder came to light,
    That showed the rogues they lied;
The man recovered of the bite,
    The dog it was that died.

                Oliver Goldsmith

Sandra Slater

Here lies what's left of Sandra Slater
Who poked her pet—an alligator—
Forgetting that to tease or bait her
Might annoy an alligator
Alas the alligator ate her.

John Foster

Don't Call Alligator Long-Mouth Till You Cross River

Call alligator long-mouth
call alligator saw-mouth
call alligator pushy-mouth
call alligator scissors-mouth
call alligator raggedy-mouth
call alligator bumpy-bum
call alligator all dem rude word
but better wait
           till you cross river

                           John Agard

Don't Let Your Gerbil Out of the Cage!

Gerbil Gerry made a mess
When he got trapped in the trouser press.
It's sad to say, the truth is that
Both of us now feel quite flat.
Poor old pet with a permanent crease,
Gerry Gerbil, *Pressed in Peace*.

Andrew Fusek Peters

Revenge of the Hamster

No one realized, nobody knew
The hamster was sleeping inside my dad's shoe.

He put in his foot and squashed flat its nose
So it opened its jaws and chomped on his toes.

While howling and yowling and hopping like mad
The hamster wreaked revenge on my dad.

It scampered and scurried up his trouser leg . . .
And this time bit something much softer instead.

His eyes bulged and popped like marbles on stalks
And watered while walking the strangest of walks.

His ears wiggled wildly while shooting out steam
All the dogs in the town heard his falsetto scream.

His face went deep purple, his hair stood on end,
His mouth like a letter box caught in the wind.

The hamster's revenge was almost complete . . .
Dad couldn't sit down for several weeks.

Now Dad doesn't give our hamster a chance . . .
He wears stainless steel socks and hamster-proof pants.

Paul Cookson

Monster

I suddenly spot it from an upstairs window—
a colossal slug, crossing the garden
from East to West. How to stop it?

Salt would make a horrible death,
there would be writhing and shrivelling, a mess.
A boulder thrown from here would be sure to miss.

It goes so slowly that I rush off
to get expert advice. I ring the gardener
who is out. When I come back

it has munched the marigolds, swallowed
the salvias, and grown to alsatian-size.
The garden is full of silvery slime.

Now it leans its whale-like bulk
against the shed. The sound of splintering wood
sends the cat shrieking over the rooftops.

I run downstairs, lock and bolt the kitchen door.

Connie Bensley

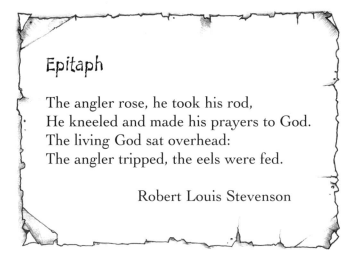

Epitaph

The angler rose, he took his rod,
He kneeled and made his prayers to God.
The living God sat overhead:
The angler tripped, the eels were fed.

Robert Louis Stevenson

Just Desserts

Jelly and custard, lemon meringue pie
Sherry trifle with cream piled high

Mincemeat tart and blackberry sponge
Roly poly with syrupy gunge

Chocolate-coated profiterole
Sugary donut (without the hole)

Pineapple fritters and crème brûlée
Treacle toffee straight from the tray

Ice cream with banana split in two
Butterscotch fudge, sticky like glue

Rhubarb crumble and strawberry cheesecake
Brandy snaps that'll make your teeth ache

Christmas pudding, just one more slice
For goodness' sake, take my advice:

If all you eat is just desserts
One day you'll get your just desserts.

Roger McGough

Miss Jessica and Sugar

Miss Jessica love sugar is a shame
Miss Jessica know every sweetie by name
Miss Jessica no 'fraid diabetes
Miss Jessica keep sucking sweeties
Miss Jessica brush off all coconut drop
Miss Jessica gwaps down soursop
Miss Jessica no have sweet tooth tho'
she lef dem dung de dentist long time ago.

Pauline Stewart

A Legend of the Northland

Away, away in the Northland,
　　Where the hours of the day are few,
And the nights are so long in winter
　　That they cannot sleep them through;

Where they harness the swift reindeer
　　To the sledges, when it snows;
And the children look like bear's cubs
　　In their funny, furry clothes:

They tell them a curious story—
　　I don't believe 'tis true;
And yet you may learn a lesson
　　If I tell the tale to you.

Once, when the good Saint Peter
　　Lived in the world below,
And walked about it, preaching,
　　Just as he did, you know,

He came to the door of a cottage,
　　In travelling round the earth,
Where a little woman was making cakes,
　　And baking them on the hearth;

And being faint with fasting,
    For the day was almost done,
He asked her, from her store of cakes,
    To give him a single one.

So she made a very little cake,
    But as it baking lay,
She looked at it, and thought it seemed
    Too large to give away.

Therefore she kneaded another,
    And still a smaller one;
But it looked, when she turned it over,
    As large as the first had done.

Then she took a tiny scrap of dough,
    And rolled and rolled it flat;
And baked it thin as a wafer —
    But she couldn't part with that.

For she said, 'My cakes that seem too small
    When I eat of them myself
Are yet too large to give away.'
    So she put them on the shelf.

Then good Saint Peter grew angry,
    For he was hungry and faint;
And surely such a woman
    Was enough to provoke a saint.

And he said, 'You are far too selfish
    To dwell in a human form,
To have both food and shelter,
    And fire to keep you warm.

'Now, you shall build as the birds do,
    And shall get your scanty food
By boring, and boring, and boring,
    All day in the hard, dry wood.'

Then up she went through the chimney,
    Never speaking a word,
And out of the top flew a woodpecker,
    For she was changed to a bird.

She had had a scarlet cap on her head,
    And that was left the same;
But all the rest of her clothes were burned
    Black as a coal in the flame.

And every country schoolboy
    Has seen her in the wood,
Where she lives in the trees till this very day,
    Boring and boring for food.

Phoebe Cary

Rules for Cooking Toast

Be accurate when cooking toast
Never try to guess
Cook it till it smokes and then
Twenty seconds less.

Anon.

Misfortunes Never Come Singly

Making toast at the fireside,
Nurse fell in the grate and died;
And what makes it ten times worse,
All the toast was burnt with nurse.

Harry Graham

The Spearmint Spuggy from Space Stuck on Every Seat in School

Spuggy on the seat
Chewy on the chair
Bubble gum gunge gets everywhere

It stands on my hands
strands expand like rubber bands.

Congeals and feels like stretch and seal
a scaly skin that you just can't peel.

It smears, here, inside my ears
and round my eyes . . . bubble gum tears.

Beware! It's there
tangled dread locks in my hair.

Look! It's stuck . . .
a pink punk starfish standing up.

It grows all over my nose
so when I breathe a bubble blows

Like polythene or Plasticine
and the bubble that blows is pink and green.

It's pale, a putrid trail
left by a rubber mutant snail
a string vest made from the blubber from a whale
a slimy slug with a six foot tail
syrup stuck on my fingernails.

It clings, like strings
of mouldy maggots and horrible things
on the end of my fingers
a big pink wriggly worm it lingers
so that you cannot distinguish
which is the gum and which are my fingers.

Splashes, splodges, blobs and blots,
blatant blotches, suspect spots,
dabs and dawbs and polka dots
multiplying lots and lots
sticky and strong it has got
the look and feel of alien snot!

Bleargh! Attishyoo!
This alien's trying to kiss you
it's getting to be an issue
one where you wish you
had more than just one Kleenex tissue.

Help! It's drastic
squeezed by snakes of pliable plastic
or an octopus with legs of elastic

Smudges on my shirt
stains on my shoe
a spider's web that's made of glue
I just don't know what to do
with this sticky icky gunged up goo
that pulls so tight my skin turns white
then a nasty ghastly shade of blue.
It's true, I haven't got a clue,
what are we going to do?
It's coming for me and it's coming for you . . .

Invasion of the body snatchers
spuggy on the seats at school will catch us,
plait, matt, attack, attach us.

It's alive, it writhes
chokes your throat and blinds your eyes.

Sticks . . . like sick
thick as an oily slick.

Exploding like a can of worms
that slither and slide and slime and squirm.

Spuggy on the seat
Chewy on the chair
Bubble gum gunge gets everywhere.

So beware! It's here and there!
Bubble gum gunge gets everywhere
and I don't know what to do
it's coming for me and it's coming for you
it's coming for me and it's coming for you
Be careful what you chew
Be careful what you chew
it may just get revenge on you
so be careful
what
you
chew

Paul Cookson

The Writer Biter

Laurie was voracious
The king of omnivores
A prisoner of plenty
A martyr to his jaws

His hunger ever present
A slave to appetite
Like a human plague of locusts
He ate everything in sight

Of verse and versifiers
He couldn't get his fill
With jaws that chomped like pliers
He moved in for the kill

One day whilst composing
On a sleepy river bank
Laurie lunged towards me
Sunk his teeth into my flank

Now Laurie's name is legion
His reputation great
Whilst I am only famous
As the poet Laurie ate.

Michael Forte

There Was a Young Lady of Ryde

There was a Young Lady of Ryde,
Who ate some green apples and died.
The apples fermented
Inside the lamented
And made cider inside her inside.

Anon.

At My Birthday Party

At my birthday party
I had chocolate cake,
And cheesecake,
And fruitcake,
And ginger cake,
And fudge cake.
After that I had stummer cake.

Anthony Browne

Ice-cream Poem

The chiefest of young Ethel's vices
Was eating multitudes of ices.

Whene'er the ice-van's booming tinkle
Was heard, Eth ran out in a twinkle,

And gorged herself on large 'Vanilla';
Her Mum foretold that it would kill 'er.

No tears could thaw her; once she ran
Away, and hid inside the van,

And promptly froze upon the spot
Like the saltpillar wife of Lot.

Poor Eth is licked! Behold the follies
Of one whose lolly went on lollies.

Though there is one thing in her favour
She now has quite a strawberry flavour.

Gerda Mayer

Puzzled

I took a sip of lemon pop
And then a sip of lime
A little orange soda, too,
A swallow at a time.
Some grape came next and cherry red,
And then I almost cried.
How *could* my stomach feel so bad
With rainbows down inside?

Margaret Hillert

Bobby's Bubble Gum

Bobby blew his bubble gum
Big and fat and wide.
Bobby blew his bubble gum
Then swallowed it inside.
The bubble gum swelled up and grew
Inside Bobby's belly
Till Bobby wobbled round the room
Like a bowl of jelly.

Bobby clutched his aching guts,
His mum began to cry;
Then Bobby sat down on a pin
And **POP!**
                He hit the sky.

So when you blow your bubble gum
Big and fat and wide:
Let it cover up your grin,
Let it dribble down your chin,
Let it cling on to your skin —
But don't swallow it inside.

Dave Ward

Greedyguts

I sat in the café and sipped at a Coke.
There sat down beside me a WHOPPING great bloke
Who sighed as he elbowed me into the wall:
'Your trouble, my boy, is your belly's too small!
Your bottom's too thin! Take a lesson from me:
I may not be nice, but I'm GREAT, you'll agree,
And I've lasted a lifetime by playing this hunch:
The bigger the breakfast, the larger the lunch!

The larger the lunch, then the huger the supper.
The deeper the teapot, the vaster the cupper.
The fatter the sausage, the fuller the tea.
The MORE on the table, the BETTER for ME!'

His elbows moved in and his elbows moved out,
His belly grew bigger, chins wobbled about,
As forkful by forkful and plate after plate,
He ate and he ate and he ate and he ATE!

I hardly could breathe, I was squashed out of shape,
So under the table I made my escape.

'Aha!' he rejoiced, 'when it's put to the test,
The fellow who's fattest will come off the best!
Remember, my boy, when it comes to the crunch:
The bigger the breakfast, the larger the lunch!

The larger the lunch, then the huger the supper.
The deeper the teapot, the vaster the cupper.
The fatter the sausage, the fuller the tea.
The MORE on the table, the BETTER for ME!'

A lady came by who was scrubbing the floor
With a mop and a bucket. To even the score,
I lifted that bucket of water and said,
As I poured the whole of it over his head:

'I've found all my life, it's a pretty sure bet:
The FULLER the bucket, the WETTER you GET!'

Kit Wright

Gregory Gruber

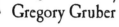

Gregory Gruber, gargantuan glutton
would gobble green gooseberries, gumbo and mutton.
He'd gurgle down gravy, gulp garlic galore
then like a great gannet, would gullet some more.
'Oh, glorious grub,' he would gasp. 'Give me grease,
give me gobstoppers, gristle. (He gave us no peace.)
Give me gollops of gruel and gobbets of goose,
grill it and garnish it, glaze it. And juice,
give me gallons and gallons to gulp and to glug
and give it to me in a gardener's trug.'
Gregory Gruber grew gross as he guzzled.
Poor Gregory Gruber should've been muzzled
for that great gourmadister's gut overloaded
and Gregory Gruber (we warned him) exploded.

Marian Swinger

Henry King, Who Chewed Bits of String, and Was Early Cut Off in Dreadful Agonies

The Chief Defect of Henry King
Was chewing little bits of String.
At last he swallowed some which tied
Itself in ugly Knots inside.
Physicians of the Utmost Fame
Were called at once; but when they came
They answered, as they took their Fees,
'There is no Cure for this Disease.
Henry will very soon be dead.'
His Parents stood about his Bed
Lamenting his Untimely Death,
When Henry, with his Latest Breath,
Cried—'Oh, my Friends, be warned by me,
That Breakfast, Dinner, Lunch and Tea
Are all the Human Frame requires . . .'
With that, the Wretched Child expires.

Hilaire Belloc

The Story of Rick, Who Ate Too Many Cheeseburgers, and What Happened to Him

Rick idled about on a sofa all day,
He couldn't be bothered to go out and play.
His friends said 'Go walking, or take up a sport!'
But Rick just replied with this savage retort,

'Shut up and push off! I'll do what I please —
Watching the telly and eating burgers with cheese!'

Now Rick's brother Christopher, (shortened to Kit)
Was horribly healthy and fearsomely fit,
It was all footie, and rugger and cricket with him,
Or sweating a lot lifting weights at the gym.

'You really must try to get fitter,' Kit said,
'If you don't, my dear brother, you'll soon end up dead.
Your heart will give out if you leave it too late,
Or your knees will start buckling under your weight!'

At last he convinced him to give it a try.
'So what should I do?' Rick asked with a sigh.
'An hour's gentle jogging will do for a start,
It won't tire you out and it's good for your heart.'

So off they went jogging. It was tough work for Rick,
'I think that last cheeseburger's making me sick!'
Down the streets of the city ran Kit in the lead,
With Rick like a hippo fast running to seed.
Kit turned to his brother. 'Get a move on,' he said,
Which was why he didn't see the great hole up ahead.

When mending a sewer or fixing a drain
The cover should always be put back again . . .
You've guessed it, in less time than it takes to tell,
With a scream and a gurgle down the manhole Kit fell.

Now if that fit lad hadn't been quite so thin,
There would have been no chance of him falling in;
Healthy living had done for him, you'll be grief-struck
    to know
He was eaten by crocodiles lurking below.

Rick puffed and he panted, but he got there at last
And fell down the same drain, but *his* stomach stuck fast,
'Help me! I'm wedged!' Someone soon heard him shout,
So they called up a crane and at last had him out.

Some stories have morals, or so it is said,
While some have no lesson, they're just there to be read:
Rick's learnt a hard lesson, through his grief and his
    pain—
If you must go out jogging, keep your eye on the drains.

David Orme

Winifred Weasel

Miss Winifred Weasel long and thin
All night sneaked around the farm,
Until she came to a narrow gap,
Newly opened in the barn.

Winifred Weasel long and thin
Squeezed her frame neatly in!

Miss Winifred Weasel felt at ease.
She was quite amazed at all she saw:
She attacked the carrots and the cheese,
And kept one eye upon the door.

Winifred Weasel long and thin
Squeezed her frame neatly in!

Miss Winifred Weasel nibbled and gnawed.
Rotund, then fat soon she grew,
And when the mouse came it deplored
How she had eaten enough for two.

Winifred Weasel long and thin
Squeezed her frame neatly in!

Suddenly outside the barn
She heard the noise of human feet.
She danced about in great alarm
But could find no way to retreat.

Winifred Weasel long and thin
Squeezed her frame neatly in!

She found the place where she got in,
But now the barn had become a trap.
She wished on her life she was still thin
And could squeeze out through that narrow gap.

Winifred Weasel once long and thin
Doomed by greed to be caged in!

Brian Patten

Hot Food

We sit down to eat
and the potato's a bit hot
so I only put a little bit on my fork
and I blow
whooph whooph
until it's cool
just cool
then into the mouth
nice.
And there's my brother
he's doing the same
whooph whooph
into the mouth
nice.
There's my mum
she's doing the same
whooph whooph
into the mouth
nice.

But my dad.
My dad.
What does he do?
He stuffs a great big chunk of potato
into his mouth,
then
that really does it.
His eyes pop out
he flaps his hands
he blows, he puffs, he yells
he bobs his head up and down
he spits bits of potato
all over his plate
and he turns to us and he says,
'Watch out everybody—
the potato's very hot.'

Michael Rosen

The Tummy Beast

One afternoon I said to mummy,
'Who is this person in my tummy?
He must be very small and very thin
Or how could he have gotten in?'
My mother said from where she sat,
'It isn't nice to talk like that.'
'It's true!' I cried. 'I swear it, mummy!
There *is* a person in my tummy!
He talks to me at night in bed,
He's always asking to be fed,
Throughout the day, he screams at me,
Demanding sugar buns for tea.
He tells me it is not a sin
To go and raid the biscuit tin.
I know quite well it's awfully wrong
To guzzle food the whole day long,
But really I can't help it, mummy,
Not with this person in my tummy!'
'You horrid child!' my mother cried.
'Admit it right away, you've lied!
You're simply trying to produce
A silly asinine excuse!
You are the greedy guzzling brat!
And that is why you're always fat!'
I tried once more, '*Believe me*, mummy,
There *is* a person in my tummy.'

'I've had enough!' my mother said,
'You'd better go at once to bed!'
Just then, a nicely timed event
Delivered me from punishment.
Deep in my tummy something stirred,
And then an awful noise was heard,
A snorting grumbling grunting sound
That made my tummy jump around.
My darling mother nearly died,
'My goodness, what was that?' she cried.
At once, the tummy voice came through,
It shouted, 'Hey there! Listen you!
I'm getting hungry! I want eats!
I want lots of chocs and sweets!
Get me half a pound of nuts!
Look snappy or I'll twist your guts!'
'That's him!' I cried. *'He's in my tummy!*
So now do you believe me, mummy?'

But mummy answered nothing more,
For she had fainted on the floor.

Roald Dahl

Roll Up, Roll Up

They had to take the Dragon Ride
At the new amusement park
They did it for a double-dare
They did it for a lark,

They'd been told the Dragon was
The best ride of the lot
A bit like being shipwrecked,
A bit like being shot,

Like being in a playground-fight
Or being sent to war:
That's why they took the Dragon,
That's what they went there for.

The ride began quite slowly
As 'coasters always do
It creaked up to the pinnacle,
So that was nothing new,

It paused a moment at the top,
The structure seemed to sway,
The drop was nearly vertical,
It took their breath away

Just to look down at the ground—
A tiny raree-show,
And them up in the clouds beside
The kestrel and the crow.

Then the Dragon took the plunge
The point of no return.
They felt their eyeballs dimple
And their lungs begin to burn,

A wicked whiplash flicked and furled
And snapped along their backs;
The Dragon's wheels were just a blur
That barely touched the tracks,

It either took a nano-second
Or it took a year,
A sky-high drop amid a slop
Of flatulence and fear,

And all the scarier because
They'd make the dip and then
The ride would slow and start to climb
And take them up again

With a chatter and a clatter and
A rattle like a geiger—
Counter to a slope just like
The north face of the Eiger . . .

Except that's not what happened.
They never felt the swerve
And sway a roller-coaster makes
When it swoops into the curve—

A flash of dragon red, a trail
Of smoke, and when it cleared
The 'coaster and the children had
Completely disappeared.

Eye-witnesses were all agreed
There was no way of knowing
How it hit the curve, but then
Just seemed to keep on going.

The ride's abandoned now, the tracks
Are rusty, and the screams
Of roller coaster riders fade
Like roller-coaster dreams

And no one now remembers
That day of endless fun
When the Dragon Ride stopped dead. Or else
Had only just begun . . .

David Harsent

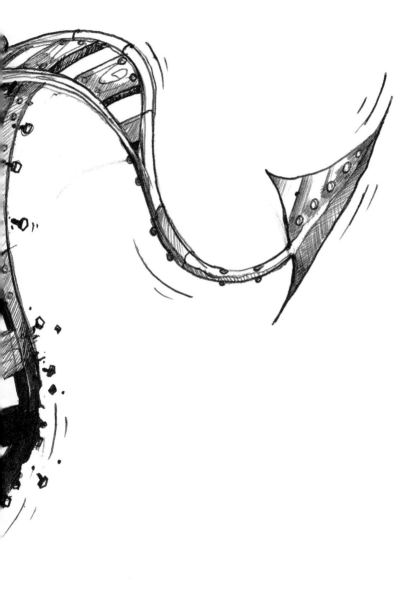

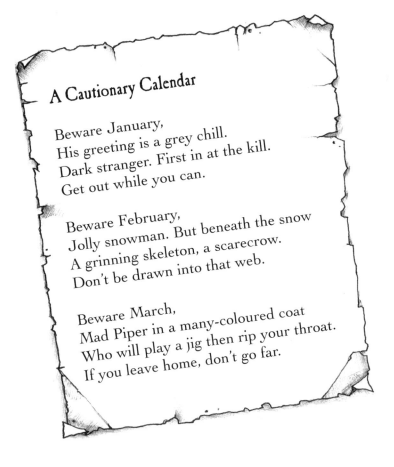

A Cautionary Calendar

Beware January,
His greeting is a grey chill.
Dark stranger. First in at the kill.
Get out while you can.

Beware February,
Jolly snowman. But beneath the snow
A grinning skeleton, a scarecrow.
Don't be drawn into that web.

Beware March,
Mad Piper in a many-coloured coat
Who will play a jig then rip your throat.
If you leave home, don't go far.

Beware April,
Who sucks eggs and tramples nests.
From the wind that molests
There is no escape.

Beware May,
Darling scalpel, gall and wormwood.
Scented blossom hides the smell
Of blood. Keep away.

Beware June,
Black lipstick, bruise-coloured rouge,
Sirensong and subterfuge.
The wide-eyed crazed hypnotic moon.

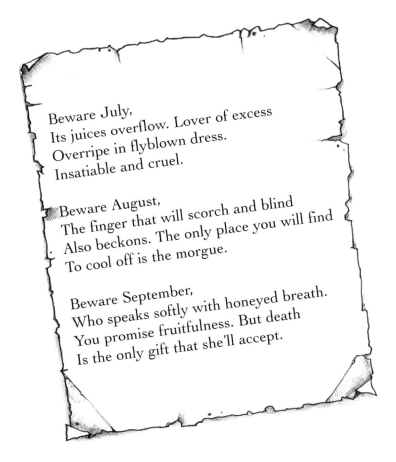

Beware July,
Its juices overflow. Lover of excess
Overripe in flyblown dress.
Insatiable and cruel.

Beware August,
The finger that will scorch and blind
Also beckons. The only place you will find
To cool off is the morgue.

Beware September,
Who speaks softly with honeyed breath.
You promise fruitfulness. But death
Is the only gift that she'll accept.

Beware October,
Whose scythe is keenest. The old crone
Makes the earth tremble and moan.
She's mean and won't be mocked.

Beware November,
Whose teeth are sharpened on cemetery stones,
Who will trip you up and crunch your bones.
Iron fist in iron glove.

Beware December,
False beard that hides a sneer.
Child-hater. In what year
Will we know peace?

Roger McGough

142

Index of poets

Acknowledgements

Every effort has been made to trace and contact copyright holders before publication and we are grateful to all those who have granted us permission. We apologize for any inadvertent errors and will be pleased to rectify these at the earliest opportunity.

John Agard: 'Don't Call Alligator Long-Mouth Till You Cross River' copyright © 1986 by John Agard, reproduced by kind permission of John Agard, c/o Caroline Sheldon Literary Agency Ltd. **Jez Alborough:** 'Ear Popping' © Jez Alborough. **David Bateman:** 'Sun, Sand And Sea' copyright © David Bateman 2004, from *Poems to Take on Holiday* OUP, reproduced by permission of the author. **Hilaire Belloc:** 'George', 'Rebecca', and 'Henry King' from *Cautionary Verses* by Hilaire Belloc (© Hilaire Belloc) is reproduced by permission of PFD (www.pfd.co,uk) on behalf of Hilaire Belloc. **Connie Bensley:** 'Monster' © Connie Bensley, reproduced by permission of the author. **Phil Bowen:** 'Timing' © Phil Bowen, reproduced by permission of the author. **Anthony Browne:** 'At My Birthday Party' © Anthony Browne, reproduced by permission of the author. **Paul Cookson:** 'Revenge of the Hamster', and 'The Spearmint Spuggy from Space Stuck on Every Seat in School' © Paul Cookson, reproduced by permission of the author. **Roald Dahl:** 'The Tummy Beast' © Roald Dahl, from *Dirty Beasts*, Jonathan Cape, reproduced by permission of David Higham Associates Ltd. **Peter Dixon:** 'Icarus' © Peter Dixon, from *The Tortoise Had a Mighty Roar*, reproduced by permission of the author. **Carol Ann Duffy:** 'Be Very Afraid' © Carol Ann Duffy, from *The Hat*, Faber 2007, reproduced by permission of the author, c/o Rogers, Coleridge & White Ltd., 20 Powis Mews, London W11 1JN. **Richard Edwards:** 'Just for Fun' from *Why Does My Mum Always Iron a Crease in My Jeans* Puffin 2005, and 'Cy's Mother Said' © Richard Edwards, reproduced by permission of the author. **Eleanor Farjeon:** 'The Witch! The Witch!' © Eleanor Farjeon, from *Silver Sand and Snows*, Michael Joseph, reproduced by permission of David Higham Associates Ltd. **Michael Forte:** 'The Writer Biter' © Michael Forte, reproduced by permission of the author. **John Foster:** 'Sandra Slater' © John Foster 2000, from *Pet Poems* OUP, included by permission of the author. **David Greygoose:** 'Where the Blackberries Grow' © David Greygoose, reproduced by permission of the author. **David Harmer:** 'Sir Guy and the Enchanted Princess' © David Harmer, reproduced by permission of the author. **David Harsent:** 'Roll Up, Roll Up' © David Harsent, reproduced by permission of the author. **Stewart Henderson:** 'No Trespassers' © Stewart Henderson, reproduced by permission of the author. **Margaret Hillert:** 'Puzzled' © Margaret Hillert, reproduced by permission of the author, who controls all rights. **Dick King-Smith:** 'Robert Jobbins', and 'Willie White' © Dick King-Smith, from *Dirty Gertie Mackintosh*, Transworld, 1996, reproduced by permission of A P Watt Ltd on behalf of Fox Busters Ltd. **Gerda Mayer:** 'Ice-cream Poem' © Gerda Mayer, from *The New Statesman*'s Weekend Comp 1958, reproduced by permission of the author.

Roger McGough: 'Cautionary Tale', 'The Boy with a Similar Name', 'Lucky', 'The Tongue-Twister', 'Just Desserts', and 'A Cautionary Calendar' © Roger McGough, reproduced by permission of the author. **Ian McMillan:** 'Cautionary Playground Rhyme' © Ian McMillan, reproduced by permission of the author. **Eve Merriam:** 'Teevee' © 1966, copyright renewed 1994 by Eve Merriam, from *Catch A Little Rhyme* by Eve Merriam. Used by permission of Marian Reiner. **Spike Milligan:** 'Bump!' © Spike Milligan, from *Beaver Book of Creepy Verse*, reproduced by kind permission of Spike Milligan Productions Ltd. **Adrian Mitchell:** 'Icarus Schmicarus' © Adrian Mitchell, reproduced by permission of the author. Education Health Warning! Adrian Mitchell asks that none of his poems are used in connection with any examinations whatsoever. **David Orme:** 'The Story of Rick, Who Ate Too Many Cheeseburgers, and What Happened to Him' © David Orme, reproduced by permission of the author. **Brian Patten:** 'Winifred Weasel' © Brian Patten, reproduced by permission of the author, c/o Rogers, Coleridge & White Ltd., 20 Powis Mews, London W11 1JN. **Andrew Fusek Peters:** 'Don't Let Your Gerbil Out of the Cage!' © Andrew Fusek Peters, from *Mad, Bad and Dangerously Haddock: the Best of Andrew Fusek Peters*, Lion, 2006. Used with permission of Lion Hudson plc. **Polly Peters:** 'Risk Assessment' © Polly Peters, reproduced by permission of the author. **Jack Prelutsky:** 'I Found a Four-Leaf Clover' from *The New Kid on the Block*, Greenwillow Books 1984, and 'Mother Goblin's Lullaby' © Jack Prelutsky, reproduced by permission of the author. **Michael Rosen:** 'Hot Food' from *The Hypnotiser* (© Michael Rosen 1988) is reproduced by permission of PFD (www.pfd.co.uk) on behalf of Michael Rosen. **Ian Serraillier:** 'The Visitor' © Estate of Ian Serraillier, from *A Second Poetry Book* OUP 1980, reproduced by permission of the Estate of Ian Serraillier. **Shel Silverstein:** 'Sybil the Magician's Last Show', 'Screamin' Millie', 'Headphone Harold', 'My Sneaky Cousin', and 'Jimmy Jet and His TV Set' © Shel Silverstein, reproduced by kind permission of Edite Kroll Literary Agency Inc. **Roger Stevens:** 'Treasure Trail' © Roger Stevens, from *I Did Not Eat the Goldfish*, Macmillan, reproduced by permission of the author. **Pauline Stewart:** 'Miss Jessica and Sugar' from *Singing Down the Breadfruit and Other Poems* by Pauline Stewart, published by The Bodley Head. Reprinted by permission of The Random House Group Ltd. **Jan Struther:** 'The Story of Anthony, the Boy Who Knew Too Much' © Jan Struther, reproduced by permission of Curtis Brown. **Marian Swinger:** 'Gregory Gruber' © Marian Swinger, from *Teasing Tongue Twisters*, reproduced by permission of the author. **George Szirtes:** 'Sid the Skateboarder' © George Szirtes, reproduced by permission of the author. **Nick Toczek:** 'The Boom-Boom-Boom from Susan's Room' © Nick Toczek, reproduced by permission of the author. **Dave Ward:** 'Bobby's Bubble Gum' © Dave Ward, reproduced by permission of the author. **Kit Wright:** 'Greedyguts' © Kit Wright 1981, from *Hot Dog and Other Poems* (Kestrel 1981), reproduced by permission of Penguin Books Ltd.